Angeles. He was appointed professor at the City College of New York in 1940, but after protests over Russell's liberal views on religion and marriage the appointment was annulled in court. He returned to Britain in 1944 to rejoin the faculty of Trinity College. During the 1940s and 1950s, Russell's oratory skills were heard on many BBC broadcasts, particularly The Brains Trust, where he spoke, with his customary acuity, on various topical and philosophical subjects. In 1948, Russell was invited by the BBC to deliver the inaugural Reith Lecture.

The 1950s and 1960s again saw Russell engaged in pacifist work, primarily related to nuclear disarmament and opposing the Vietnam War. The 1955 Russell–Einstein Manifesto called for nuclear disarmament and was signed by eleven of the most prominent nuclear physicists and intellectuals of the day. Russell continued to write and his celebrated *Autobiography* was published in three volumes between 1967 and 1969. He died in 1970 and was cremated in Colwyn Bay, Wales, near his home. His ashes were scattered over the Welsh mountains.

Alan Ryan was born in London in 1940 and taught for many years at Oxford, where he was a Fellow of New College and Reader in Politics. He was Professor of Politics at Princeton from 1988 to 1996, when he returned to Oxford to become Warden of New College and Professor of Political Theory until his retirement in 2009. His previous books include *The Philosophy of John Stuart Mill*, *Bertrand Russell: A Political Life* and *John Dewey and the High Tide of American Liberalism*. He is a Fellow of the British Academy.

Bertrand
Russell

What I Believe

London and New York

First published 1925
by Kegan Paul, Trench Trubner & Co Ltd, London

First published in Routledge Classics 2004
by Routledge

This edition published in Routledge Great Minds 2014
by Routledge
2 Park Square, Milton Park, Abingdon, Oxon, OX14 4RN

Routledge is an imprint of the Taylor & Francis Group, an informa business

© 1996 The Bertrand Russell Peace Foundation Ltd

© 2004, 2014 foreword, Alan Ryan

Typeset in Joanna by RefineCatch Ltd, Bungay, Suffolk
Printed by Bell & Bain Ltd, Glasgow

British Library Cataloguing in Publication Data
A catalogue record for this book is available from the British Library

ISBN 978-0-415-85476-4 (pbk)
ISBN 978-1-315-88959-7 (ebk)

Contents

A NOTE FROM THE PUBLISHER

This Routledge Great Minds edition of *What I Believe* contains a foreword by Alan Ryan that first appeared as a preface in the Routledge Classics edition published in 2004. Included in this edition are two essays by Russell that do not appear in the Routledge Classics edition, 'Why I Took to Philosophy' and 'How I Write'.

FOREWORD TO THE
ROUTLEDGE GREAT MINDS EDITION

Fifty years after reading Bertrand Russell for the first time, I read him today with mixed feelings. In the middle 1950s, his *History of Western Philosophy* was a treat to teenage schoolboys bored to death with the slog of O Level. It gave us all the weapons we needed to torment the school chaplain when he tried to explain to agnostic teenagers Aquinas's Five Ways to the knowledge of God's existence. *Why I am not a Christian* was an even more valuable weapon against authority. My house-master's belief that Russell's four marriages discredited his views on sex, God and nuclear warfare only confirmed my view that most holders of authority were bigoted, illogical and not to be taken seriously.

I have not wholly changed my mind. Russell's four marriages are irrelevant to his views on sex, God and nuclear warfare; I now think that his marital difficulties should have made him more wary about making the pursuit of happiness look *easy*, but his ideas about what the good life is wear well. He had many vices as a critic of views he disliked, and his practice was at odds with his professed principle of taking on one's opponents at their strongest points rather than their weakest. In those ways, he was less admirable than John Stuart Mill. On the other hand, he was, and is, much more fun. In particular, he wrote wonderfully; even the articles he turned out for the Hearst newspapers at fifty dollars a pop, in order to support Beacon Hill, the school that he and his second wife had created, are not only quick and clever, but thought-provoking too. If Britain took literacy seriously, teenagers would be given Russell as a model essayist.

During the First World War Russell realized that he had an extraordinary talent for lecturing to lay audiences. He was deeply opposed to the war and, as a member of the Union for Democratic Control early in the war and later as a leading figure in the No-Conscription Fellowship, he worked unceasingly to bring the war to an early end, to persuade the United States to remain neutral, and to protect conscientious objectors from abuse at the hand of the tribunals that heard their case for exemption, and from ill-treatment in prison or the army, if they ended up there. These activities cost him his lecturership at Trinity College, Cambridge, but they brought him into a new world, too.

In addition to the innumerable meetings aimed directly at bringing an end to the war and saving objectors from conscription, Russell gave a strikingly successful series of lectures on *The Principles of Social Reconstruction*. To the extent that he had a single political philosophy, it was contained in the short book that the lectures became. Much that is taken for granted in *What I Believe* is argued for at some length in *The Principles of Social*

Reconstruction. Three crucial premises are worth bringing into the light.

Russell's view of human behaviour was rooted in the empiricist tradition that held that *desire* propels all action, and that the role of reason is to tell us *how* to achieve what we are after, not *what* we should be after in the first place. Or, as Hume put it with the sharpness that Russell relished, 'reason is and ought to be the slave of the passions'. This was not an argument for 'impulsiveness' in the ordinary sense: Russell believed that we should think very hard about what we are up to, and he wanted more, and more scientifically informed, reflection on what we ought to do with our lives. It was an argument for trying to understand what it is that we do really want. Russell's views about the basis of our desires went farther than that. He was well acquainted with the work of W. H. Rivers, the psychiatrist who treated Siegfried Sassoon – and many others – for shell shock, and who was one of the first people in England to take the measure of Freud. Rivers thought Freud exaggerated his insights, but had no doubt that we are all much more at the mercy of hidden impulses than we like to think. So did Russell.

In particular, Russell came close to believing that human beings were instinctively impelled to destruction for its own sake, something that Freud's account of the 'death wish' also suggests. It was so obvious to him that war between nation states was unnecessary, and therefore deeply stupid, that he found it hard to believe that anything could explain it other than a passion for destruction and a desire by the combatants to inflict suffering on others at no matter what price in suffering for themselves. To believe anything so nihilistic, however, would have made Russell's pacifism futile. If we are determined to destroy ourselves for no good reason, the only interesting question is how long it will be before we find the technology to wipe ourselves out completely. Russell was always ready for rhetorical purposes to represent his opponents as imbued with a passion to commit mass murder and mass suicide, but in his more analytical moments, he proposed a different and more elaborate view.

This view was the second premise of his politics. He argued in *Principles* that there are two kinds of impulse; the *possessive* impulse seeks exclusive ownership of whatever it lights on, and leads us to compete with each other, while the *creative* impulse leads us to look for things that can be had by one person without anyone else being any the worse for it. If German scientists discover dazzling new theorems in physics, it leaves no fewer dazzling new theorems to be discovered by French and British scientists, whereas the German seizure of South West Africa leaves so much the less territory for the French and British, to say nothing of the original inhabitants. If possessiveness gets attached to national glory, and national glory is then conceived as requiring the humiliation of other nations, we have the recipe for endless wars. Peace and happiness can only be secured by encouraging the creative instincts and diverting the possessive instincts to useful or at any rate harmless ends.

Third, then, come the ethics that Russell found it in himself to preach. As a matter of logic in the narrowest sense, Russell's ethics owe nothing to his larger philosophical views. This is a point he made for himself innumerable times. Strictly, he said, there could be no philosophical defence of any particular morality; philosophy is concerned with issues in which *truth* is at stake. Moral judgement is exhortation, encouragement, reproach – the expression of attitudes in favour of or hostile to whatever action, or character trait might be under discussion. 'Murder is evil' does not state a property of murder; it denounces murder. Moral philosophy is not philosophy at all. This was a dramatic way to make a familiar point. Russell often offered analyses of the logic of moral utterances that are unequivocally philosophical in the modern sense. It is, however, easy to see what drove Russell. For a long time, he held that even the most abstract branches of philosophy – logic and the foundations of mathematics included – are concerned to show the world as it really is. Morality's concern is with how the world should be rather than with how it is.

Given all that, Russell's ethical theory is unsurprising. Our impulses in themselves are neither good nor bad; they are brute facts. They are good and bad according to the way they assist or frustrate other impulses, either our own or those of other people. My desire to drink myself silly is just a desire, but it is at odds with my desire to wake up without a hangover; it is at odds with your desire to travel the roads safely, as well as with my employer's desire to have a coherent receptionist in the front office. Drinking oneself silly is at best imprudent and in many circumstances wicked. The wish to be helpful and co-operative on the other hand, assists others to realize their goals and will not impede my other desires. We therefore call benevolence, helpfulness and kindness good. Our standards of prudent and morally acceptable behaviour rest on our assessment of what Russell later called the 'compossibility' of desire. We should cultivate those desires that assist in the satisfaction of desires and eliminate those that frustrate them.

The connection with Russell's account of the creative instincts, and his hatred of the war hardly needs labouring. Nor does the fact that couching his account of ethics in terms of desire-satisfaction seems to provide the basis for a secular, naturalistic, and hedonistic moral theory. It is arguable that if Russell had been consistent, this is what he would have offered his readers. In fact, he did not; what emerged was secular and naturalistic, but not (mostly) a defence of hedonism. Very much like his godfather, John Stuart Mill, Russell stood up for high ideals that are only loosely connected to the pursuit of happiness in any everyday sense – courage, for instance, the love of truth, and a non-instrumental concern for the natural world among them. Rightly or wrongly, Russell agreed with Mill that Socrates dissatisfied is a better man than the fool satisfied. *What I Believe* defends the disinterested pursuit of the truth as one element in the good life, and Russell's most passionate complaint against religion is that it is a *cowardly* response to the bleakness of the universe.

What I Believe appeared in a series of very short books – the publishers described them as 'Pamphlets' – called 'Today and Tomorrow'. They were very short books on very large subjects: 'the future of Women, War, Population, Science, Machines, Morals, Drama, Poetry, Art, Music, Sex, etc.' Dora Russell wrote *Hypatia* in defence of women's liberation and Russell wrote two pamphlets in the series, of which *What I Believe* was the second. J. B. S. Haldane's *Daedalus*, had offered an optimistic view of what science would do for humanity in the future; Russell riposted with *Icarus*, to point out that Daedalus's son learned how to fly, but not how to fly intelligently. Since science as the fruit of rational inquiry into the world could only tell us *how* to achieve our goals, it was all too likely that the most impressive result of scientific advance would be to turn warfare into global massacre. If we avoided that fate, we would either find ourselves bored to death as large scale bureaucracies took over the management of the world, or be turned into the docile creatures imagined in Huxley's *Brave New World* – a book that was probably inspired by Russell's *Icarus* – genetically engineered to fit into our social roles, and fed drugs that would achieve whatever eugenics had not.

Because Russell was one of the founders of the Campaign for Nuclear Disarmament, and a prolific writer on the horrors of nuclear warfare, it is easy to forget that his fears for the future of humanity were not first aroused by nuclear weapons, but by the industrialized warfare of the First World War, and then by the advent of the long-range bomber in the 1930s. *Icarus* was mordant in its wit, savagely unfair in its characterization of almost all holders of power as wicked and reckless, and deeply pessimistic about the prospects of the human race. Not for the last time did Russell express the view that it might be a good thing for humanity to exterminate itself, since it made such a mess of existence.

What I Believe was avowedly intended to redress the balance. It is so lucid and so amusing that explaining its contents to a reader about to have the pleasure of reading Russell for themselves seems foolish. What may be more helpful is to say a little about Russell's characteristic stance on matters of religion, and about the decidedly upbeat conclusion of *What I Believe*, in which the productive rather than the destructive possibilities of science are broached as a counter to the gloom of *Icarus*.

There are two sorts of atheist – Russell called himself an agnostic to indicate that it was not impossible that there should be some sort of God, but he was perfectly certain that God did not exist, and atheist seems more apt. The position of the first sort of atheist is sometimes paraphrased as 'there is no God, and I hate him'; he or she wishes that there was a God, in order to have someone to complain at about the absurdity of the universe. Leonard Woolf once remarked that he would like to question God about the design of the human digestive system, the plumbing of which seemed peculiarly inept. The second sort of atheist is more bored than outraged; he or she cannot see what purpose is served by inventing stories about gods, spirits, or whatever supernatural entities you care to name; they add nothing to our understanding of the world, and bring with them intellectual clutter and grounds for mutual persecution when our species hardly needs to be encouraged in its incoherence and violence. One can be both sorts, but it is rhetorically awkward to be both at once.

Russell was as often the first sort of atheist as the second, but *What I Believe* is mostly written from this second point of view. All the same, it is the first sort of atheism that supplies much of the emotional force even of this essay. Atheists who cannot see why anyone would bother to invent unbelievable stories about the origins of the universe and how we are supposed to behave, might be expected to say nothing on the subject and to devote themselves to other matters. Russell rarely passed up an opportunity to speak unkindly about the devout – and was repaid in kind.

The obvious explanation is that Russell was at least half convinced that human existence was a miserable business; life could have been wonderful, but very largely was not. It was therefore intolerable to think that some being might deliberately have created a world in which we suffer constant anxiety, die of painful diseases when we do not die of violence, and suffer vastly more acute pains from heartbreak and disappointment than the pleasures of love and realized ambition can justify. If there were a God, he, she, it, or they should be tried for crimes against humanity. The devout are guilty of praising wickedness, either because they are too cowardly to face the fact that God is a criminal, or because they have a perverted sense of morality and really believe that might makes right.

The atheism of *What I Believe* is of the less inflamed, second kind. What there is to be known about the world is what science reveals, and there is no good reason to suppose either that we are immortal, or that some ghostly clockmaker stands behind the machinery of the universe. Nonetheless, some sharp complaints are levelled at the role of religion in ethics and politics. Russell particularly seizes the occasion to denounce the religious for advocating birth control by war and famine while trying to prevent birth control using contraception as advocated by Margaret Sanger and others at the time. Russell, of course, took a delight in enraging the devout by arguments such as these. Many of his readers deplore his frequent unfairness, but there was a serious point behind his rhetorical tactics.

It is this: many religions – Christianity particularly – pay an obsessive attention to matters of sexual conduct. Instead of asking what would allow people to lead tolerably happy lives, bring up enough, but not too many, healthy, happy and decently educated children, Christians, in Russell's view, spend their time making it harder rather than easier to think about such things calmly. Looking at the opponents of abortion in the United States almost eighty years later, it is easy to sympathize with Russell. The godly got their revenge on Russell in 1940, when a New York court overturned his appointment at City College on the grounds that he taught 'immorality'. *What I Believe* was part of the evidence his enemies appealed to.

At least one of Russell's objections to religiously based moralities would apply to more than those moralities which are based on religion, narrowly defined. Russell was hostile to all forms of ethics based on rules. Rightly enough, Russell thought morality plays a very small part in life. Nobody looks up the rules about parental duty when caring for a sick child, for instance; they are motivated by love – or not – and in either event morality plays no role. If they lack proper affection, they will not be moralized into it, and if they feel it, the moral standpoint is redundant. Russell was especially hostile to the thought that morality consists of rules laid down by some authority, whether God or the superego. Rules are inflexible, and the one thing Russell was sure of was that intelligent thought about our conduct must have a flexibility that matched the changeability of events.

Finally, then, the role of science in all this. In *What I Believe*, Russell said firmly that we should not 'respect' nature but learn how nature works so as to turn nature's powers to useful human ends. There are two things to be said about this. First, as we have seen, Russell was in two minds about whether humanity had the sense to use science for good ends rather than bad; the tendency in *Icarus* is to dwell on the probability that we shall misuse science, but in *What I Believe* it is to exhort us to use it for good ends. Secondly, Russell relies very heavily on the contrast between religion and morality conceived as inflexible rules that lack any rational basis or gratify the human taste for cruelty, and science conceived as the piece-meal understanding of what causes what on the other. The scientific attitude is what he wants to foster.

He was not always eager to tell his readers not to respect nature. Forty years later he commented bitterly on the eagerness of mankind to defile the heavens by putting into orbit satellites that would launch nuclear warheads at the enemy, and he accused the American pragmatist John Dewey of 'impiety' in suggesting that nature was somehow infused with human purpose. This is not a simple contradiction. At no time did Russell think that nature provided a moral standard or was itself a source of norms for our conduct; when he denounces 'respect' in *What I Believe*, that is the point he is making. At the same time he always found the vast emptiness of the universe deeply moving – terrifying and consoling at the same time. That emotion has led many readers to decide that Russell was despite himself a deeply religious thinker. If so, he was one of many religious thinkers who have found all actual religions repulsively inadequate to the sentiments they purport to express.

2003   ALAN RYAN

PREFACE

In this little book, I have tried to say what I think of man's place in the universe, and of his possibilities in the way of achieving the good life. In *Icarus* I expressed my fears; in the following pages I have expressed my hopes. The inconsistency is only apparent. Except in astronomy, mankind have not achieved the art of predicting the future; in human affairs, we can see that there are forces making for happiness, and forces making for misery. We do not know which will prevail, but to act wisely we must be aware of both.

January, 1st 1925   B. R.

1

NATURE AND MAN

Man is a part of Nature, not something contrasted with Nature. His thoughts and his bodily movements follow the same laws that describe the motions of stars and atoms. The physical world is large compared with Man – larger than it was thought to be in Dante's time, but not so large as it seemed a hundred years ago. Both upward and downward, both in the large and in the small, science seems to be reaching limits. It is thought that the universe is of finite extent in space, and that light could travel round it in a few hundred millions of years. It is thought matter consists of electrons and protons, which are of finite size and of which there are only a finite number in the world. Probably their changes are not continuous, as used to be thought, but proceed by jerks, which are never smaller than a certain minimum jerk. The laws of these changes can apparently be summed up in a small number of very general principles, which determine the past and the future of the world when any small section of its history is known.

Physical science is thus approaching the stage when it will be complete, and therefore uninteresting. Given the laws governing the motions of electrons and protons, the rest is merely geography – a collection of particular facts telling their distribution throughout some portion of the world's history. The total number of facts of geography required to determine the world's history is probably finite; theoretically they could all be written down in a big book to be kept at Somerset House with a calculating machine attached which, by turning a handle, would enable the inquirer to find out the facts at other times than those recorded. It is difficult to imagine anything less interesting or more different from the passionate delights of incomplete discovery. It is like climbing a high mountain and finding nothing at the top except a restaurant where they sell ginger beer, surrounded by fog but equipped with wireless. Perhaps in the times of Ahmes the multiplication table was exciting.

Of this physical world, uninteresting in itself, Man is a part. His body, like other matter, is composed of electrons and protons, which, so far as we know, obey the same laws as those not forming part of animals or plants. There are some who maintain that physiology can never be reduced to physics, but their arguments are not very convincing and it seems prudent to suppose that they are mistaken. What we call our 'thoughts' seem to depend upon the organisation of tracks in the brain in the same sort of way in which journeys depend upon roads and railways. The energy used in thinking seems to have a chemical origin; for instance, a deficiency of iodine will turn a clever man into an idiot. Mental phenomena seem to be bound up with material structure. If this be so, we cannot suppose that a solitary electron or proton can 'think'; we might as well expect a solitary individual to play a football match. We also cannot suppose that an individual's thinking survives bodily death, since that destroys the organisation of the brain, and dissipates the energy which utilised the brain tracks.

God and immortality, the central dogmas of the Christian religion, find no support in science. It cannot be said that either doctrine is essential to religion, since neither is found in Buddhism. (With regard to immortality, this statement in an unqualified form might be misleading, but it is correct in the last analysis.) But we in the West have come to think of them as the irreducible minimum of theology. No doubt people will continue to entertain these beliefs, because they are pleasant, just as it is pleasant to think ourselves virtuous and our enemies wicked. But for my part I cannot see any ground for either. I do not pretend to be able to prove that there is no God. I equally cannot prove that Satan is a fiction. The Christian God may exist; so may the Gods of Olympus, or of ancient Egypt, or of Babylon. But no one of these hypotheses is more probable than any other: they lie outside the region of even probable knowledge, and therefore there is no reason to consider any of them. I shall not enlarge upon this question, as I have dealt with it elsewhere.[1]

The question of personal immortality stands on a somewhat different footing. Here evidence either way is possible. Persons are part of the everyday world with which science is concerned, and the conditions which determine their existence are discoverable. A drop of water is not immortal; it can be resolved into oxygen and hydrogen. If, therefore, a drop of

---

[1] See my *Philosophy of Leibniz*, Chapter XV.

water were to maintain that it had a quality of aqueousness which would survive its dissolution we should be inclined to be sceptical. In like manner we know that the brain is not immortal, and that the organised energy of a living body becomes, as it were, demobilised at death, and therefore not available for collective action. All the evidence goes to show that what we regard as our mental life is bound up with brain structure and organised bodily energy. Therefore it is rational to suppose that mental life ceases when bodily life ceases. The argument is only one of probability, but it is as strong as those upon which most scientific conclusions are based.

There are various grounds upon which this conclusion might be attacked. Psychical research professes to have actual scientific evidence of survival, and undoubtedly its procedure is, in principle, scientifically correct. Evidence of this sort might be so overwhelming that no one with a scientific temper could reject it. The weight to be attached to the evidence, however, must depend upon the antecedent probability of the hypothesis of survival. There are always different ways of accounting for any set of phenomena and of these we should prefer the one which is antecedentally least improbable. Those who already think it likely that we survive death will be ready to view this theory as the best explanation of psychical phenomena. Those who, on other grounds, regard this theory as implausible will seek for other explanations. For my part, I consider the evidence so far adduced by psychical research in favour of survival much weaker than the physiological evidence on the other side. But I fully admit that it might at any moment become stronger, and in that case it would be unscientific to disbelieve in survival.

Survival of bodily death is, however, a different matter from immortality: it may only mean a postponement of psychical death. It is immortality that men desire to believe in. Believers in immortality will object to physiological arguments, such as I have been using, on the ground that soul and body are totally disparate, and that the soul is something quite other than its empirical manifestations through our bodily organs. I believe this to be a metaphysical superstition. Mind and matter alike are for certain purposes convenient terms, but are not ultimate realities. Electrons and protons, like the soul, are logical fictions; each is really a history, a series of events, not a single persistent entity. In the case of the soul, this is obvious from the facts of growth. Whoever considers conception, gestation, and infancy cannot seriously believe that the soul in any indivisible something, perfect and complete throughout this process. It is evident that it grows like the body, and that it derives both from the spermatozoon and from the ovum, so that it cannot be indivisible. This is not materialism: it is merely the recognition that everything interesting is a matter of organisation, not of primal substance.

Metaphysicians have advanced innumerable arguments to prove that the soul must be immortal. There is one simple test by which all these arguments can be demolished. They all prove equally that the soul must pervade all space. But as we are not so anxious to be fat as to live long, none of the metaphysicians in question have ever noticed this application of their reasonings. This is an instance of the amazing power of desire in blinding even very able men to fallacies which would otherwise be obvious at once. If we were not afraid of death, I do not believe that the idea of immortality would ever have arisen.

Fear is the basis of religious dogma, as of so much else in human life. Fear of human beings, individually or collectively, dominates much of our social life, but it is fear of nature that gives rise to religion. The antithesis of mind and matter is, as we have seen, more or less illusory; but there is another antithesis which is more important – that, namely, between things that can be affected by our desires and things that cannot be so affected. The line between the two is neither sharp nor immutable – as science advances, more and more things are brought under human control. Nevertheless there remain things definitely on the other side. Among these are all the *large* facts of our world, the sort of facts that are dealt with by astronomy. It is only facts on or near the surface of the earth that we can, to some extent, mould to suit our desires. And even on the surface of the earth our powers are very limited. Above all, we cannot prevent death, although we can often delay it.

Religion is an attempt to overcome this antithesis. If the world is controlled by God, and God can be moved by prayer, we acquire a share in omnipotence. In former days, miracles happened in answer to prayer; they still do in the Catholic Church, but Protestants have lost this power. However, it is possible to dispense with miracles, since Providence has decreed that the operation of natural laws shall produce the best possible results. Thus belief in God still serves to human-ise the world of nature, and to make men feel that physical forces are really their allies. In like manner immortality removes the terror from death. People who believe that when they die they will inherit eternal bliss may be expected to view death without horror, though, fortunately for medical men, this does not invariably happen. It does, however, soothe men's fears somewhat even when it cannot allay them wholly.

Religion, since it has its source in terror, has dignified certain kinds of fear, and made people think them not dis-graceful. In this it has done mankind a great disservice: *all* fear is bad. I believe that when I die I shall rot, and nothing of my ego will survive. I am not young, and I love life. But I should scorn to shiver with terror at the thought of annihilation. Happiness is none the less true happiness because it must come to an end, nor do thought and love lose their value because they are not everlasting. Many a man has borne himself proudly on the scaffold; surely the same pride should teach us to think truly about man's place in the world. Even if the open windows of science at first make us shiver after the cosy indoor warmth of traditional humanising myths, in the end the fresh air brings vigour, and the great spaces have a splendour of their own.

The philosophy of nature is one thing, the philosophy of value is quite another. Nothing but harm can come of confusing them. What we think good, what we should like, has no bearing whatever upon what is, which is the question for the philosophy of nature. On the other hand, we cannot be forbidden to value this or that on the ground that the non-human world does not value it, nor can we be compelled to admire anything because it is a 'law of nature'. Undoubtedly we are part of nature, which has produced our desires, our hopes and fears, in accordance with laws which the physicist is beginning to discover. In this sense we are part of nature, we are subordinated to nature, the outcome of natural laws, and their victims in the long run.

The philosophy of nature must not be unduly terrestrial; for it, the earth is merely one of the smaller planets of one of the smaller stars of the Milky Way. It would be ridiculous to warp the philosophy of nature in order to bring out results that are pleasing to the tiny parasites of this insignificant planet. Vitalism as a philosophy, and evolutionism, show, in this respect, a lack of sense of proportion and logical relevance. They regard the facts of life, which are personally interesting to us, as having a cosmic significance, not a significance confined to the earth's surface. Optimism and pessimism, as cosmic philosophies, show the same naïve humanism; the great world, so far as we know it from the philosophy of nature, is neither good nor bad, and is not concerned to make us happy or unhappy. All such philosophies spring from self-importance, and are best corrected by a little astronomy.

But in the philosophy of value the situation is reversed. Nature is only a part of what we can imagine; everything, real or imagined, can be appraised by us, and there is no outside standard to show that our valuation is wrong. We are ourselves the ultimate and irrefutable arbiters of value, and in the world of value Nature is only a part. Thus in this world we are greater than Nature. In the world of values, Nature in itself is neutral, neither good nor bad, deserving of neither admiration nor censure. It is we who create value and our desires which confer value. In this realm we are kings, and we debase our kingship if we bow down to Nature. It is for us to determine the good life, not for Nature – not even for Nature personified as God.

2

THE GOOD LIFE

There have been at different times and among different people many varying conceptions of the good life. To some extent the differences were amenable to argument; this was when men differed as to the means to achieve a given end. Some think that prison is a good way of preventing crime; others hold that education would be better. A difference of this sort can be decided by sufficient evidence. But some differences cannot be tested in this way. Tolstoy condemned all war; others have held the life of a soldier doing battle for the right to be very noble. Here there was probably involved a real difference as to ends. Those who praise the soldier usually consider the punishment of sinners a good thing in itself; Tolstoy did not think so. On such a matter no argument is possible. I cannot, therefore, prove that my view of the good life is right; I can only state my view, and hope that as many as possible will agree. My view is this:

The good life is one inspired by love and guided by knowledge.

Knowledge and love are both indefinitely extensible; therefore, however good a life may be, a better life can be imagined. Neither love without knowledge, nor knowledge without love can produce a good life. In the Middle Ages, when pestilence appeared in a country, holy men advised the population to assemble in churches and pray for deliverance; the result was that the infection spread with extraordinary rapidity among the crowded masses of supplicants. This was an example of love, without knowledge. The late war afforded an example of knowledge without love. In each case, the result was death on a large scale.

Although both love and knowledge are necessary, love is in a sense more fundamental, since it will lead intelligent people to seek knowledge, in order to find out how to benefit those whom they love. But if people are not intelligent, they will be content to believe what they have been told, and may do harm in spite of the most genuine benevolence. Medicine affords, perhaps, the best example of what I mean. An able physician is more useful to a patient than the most devoted friend, and progress in medical knowledge does more for the health of the community than ill-informed philanthropy. Nevertheless, an element of benevolence is essential even here if any but the rich are to profit by scientific discoveries.

Love is a word which covers a variety of feelings; I have used it purposely, as I wish to include them all. Love as an emotion – which is what I am speaking about, for love 'on principle' does not seem to me genuine – moves between two poles: on one side, pure delight in contemplation; on the other, pure benevolence. Where inanimate objects are concerned, delight alone enters in; we cannot feel benevolence towards a landscape or a sonata. This type of enjoyment is presumably the source of art. It is stronger, as a rule, in very young children than in adults, who are apt to view objects in a utilitarian spirit. It plays a large part in our feelings towards human beings, some of whom have charm and some the reverse, when considered simply as objects of aesthetic contemplation.

The opposite pole of love is pure benevolence. Men have sacrificed their lives to helping lepers; in such a case the love they felt cannot have had any element of aesthetic delight. Parental affection, as a rule, is accompanied by pleasure in the child's appearance, but remains strong when this element is wholly absent. It would seem odd to call a mother's interest in a sick child 'benevolence', because we are in the habit of using this word to describe a pale emotion nine parts hum-bug. But it is difficult to find any other word to describe the desire for another person's welfare. It is a fact that a desire of this sort may reach any degree of strength in the case of parental feeling. In other cases it is far less intense; indeed it would seem likely that all altruistic emotion is a sort of over-flow of parental feeling, or sometimes a sublimation of it. For want of a better word, I shall call this emotion 'benevolence'. But I want to make it clear that I am speaking of an emotion, not a principle, and that I do not include in it any feeling of superiority such as is sometimes associated with the word. The word 'sympathy' expresses part of what I mean, but leaves out the element of activity that I wish to include.

Love at its fullest is an indissoluble combination of the two elements, delight and well-wishing. The pleasure of a parent in a beautiful and successful child combines both elements; so does sex-love at its best. But in sex-love benevolence will only exist where there is secure possession, since otherwise jealousy will destroy it, while perhaps actually increasing the delight in contemplation. Delight without well-wishing may be cruel; well-wishing without delight easily tends to become cold and a little superior. A person who wishes to be loved wishes to be the object of a love containing both elements, except in cases of extreme weakness, such as infancy and severe illness. In these cases benevolence may be all that is desired. Conversely, in cases of extreme strength, admiration is more desired than benevolence: this is the state of mind of potentates and famous beauties. We only desire other people's good wishes in proportion as we feel ourselves in need of help or in danger of harm from them. At least, that would seem to be the biological logic of the situation, but it is not quite true to life. We desire affection in order to escape from the feeling of loneliness, in order to be, as we say, 'understood'. This is a matter of sympathy, not merely of benevolence; the person whose affection is satisfactory to us must not merely wish us well, but must know in what our happiness consists. But this belongs to the other element of the good life, namely knowledge.

In a perfect world, every sentient being would be to every other the object of the fullest love, compounded of delight, benevolence, and understanding inextricably blended. It does not follow that, in this actual world, we ought to attempt to have such feelings towards all the sentient beings whom we encounter. There are many in whom we cannot feel delight, because they are disgusting; if we were to do violence to our nature by trying to see beauties in them, we should merely blunt our susceptibilities to what we naturally find beautiful. Not to mention human beings there are fleas and bugs and lice. We should have to be as hard pressed as the Ancient Mariner before we could feel delight in contemplating these creatures. Some saints, it is true, have called them 'pearls of God', but what these men delighted in was the opportunity of displaying their own sanctity.

Benevolence is easier to extend widely, but even benevolence has its limits. If a man wished to marry a lady, we should not think the better of him for withdrawing if he found that someone else also wished to marry her: we should regard this as a fair field for competition. Yet his feelings towards a rival cannot be wholly benevolent. I think that in all descriptions of the good life here on earth we must assume a certain basis of animal vitality and animal instinct; without this, life becomes tame and uninteresting. Civilisation should be something added to this, not substituted for it; the ascetic saint and the detached sage fail in this respect to be complete human beings. A small number of them may enrich a community; but a world composed of them would die of boredom.

These considerations lead to a certain emphasis on the element of delight as an ingredient in the best love. Delight, in this actual world, is unavoidably selective, and prevents us from having the same feelings towards all mankind. When conflicts arise between delight and benevolence, they must, as a rule, be decided by a compromise, not by a complete surrender of either. Instinct has its rights, and if we do violence to it beyond a point it takes vengeance in subtle ways. Therefore in aiming at a good life the limits of human possibility must be borne in mind. Here again, however, we are brought back to the necessity of knowledge.

When I speak of knowledge as an ingredient of the good life, I am not thinking of ethical knowledge, but of scientific knowledge and knowledge of particular facts. I do not think there is, strictly speaking, such a thing as ethical knowledge. If we desire to achieve some end, knowledge may show us the means, and this knowledge may loosely pass as ethical. But I do not believe that we can decide what sort of conduct is right or wrong except by reference to its probable consequences. Given an end to be achieved, it is a question for science to discover how to achieve it. All moral rules must be tested by examining whether they tend to realise ends that we desire. I say ends that we desire, not ends that we *ought* to desire. What we 'ought' to desire is merely what someone else wishes us to desire. Usually it is what the authorities wish us to desire – parents, school-masters, policemen, and judges. If you say to me 'you ought to do so-and-so', the motive power of your remark lies in my desire for your approval – together, possibly, with rewards or punishments attached to your approval or disapproval. Since all behaviour springs from desire, it is clear that ethical notions can have no importance except as they influence desire. They do this through the desire for approval and the fear of disapproval. These are powerful social forces, and we shall naturally endeavour to win them to our side if we wish to realise any social purpose. When I say that the morality of conduct is to be judged by its probable consequences, I mean that I desire to see approval given to behaviour likely to realise social purposes which we desire, and disapproval to opposite behaviour. At present this is not done; there are certain traditional rules according to which approval and disapproval are meted out quite regardless of consequences. But this is a topic with which we shall deal in the next section.

The superfluity of theoretical ethics is obvious in simple cases. Suppose, for instance, your child is ill. Love makes you wish to cure it, and science tells you how to do so. There is not an intermediate stage of ethical theory, where it is demonstrated that your child had better be cured. Your act springs directly from desire for an end, together with knowledge of means. This is equally true of all acts, whether good or bad. The ends differ, and the knowledge is more adequate in some cases than in others. But there is no conceivable way of making people do things they do not wish to do. What is possible is to alter their desires by a system of rewards and penalties, among which social approval and disapproval are not the least potent. The question for the legislative moralist is, therefore: How shall this system of rewards and punishments be arranged so as to secure the maximum of what is desired by the legislative authority? If I say that the legislative authority has bad desires, I mean merely that its desires conflict with those of some section of the community to which I belong. Outside human desires there is no moral standard.

Thus, what distinguishes ethics from science is not any special kind of knowledge but merely desire. The knowledge required in ethics is exactly like the knowledge elsewhere; what is peculiar is that certain ends are desired, and that right conduct is what conduces to them. Of course, if the definition of right conduct is to make a wide appeal, the ends must be such as large sections of mankind desire. If I defined right conduct as that which increases my own income, readers would disagree. The whole effectiveness of any ethical argument lies in its scientific part, i.e. in the proof that one kind of conduct, rather than some other, is a means to an end which is widely desired. I distinguish, however, between ethical argument and ethical education. The latter consists in strengthening certain desires and weakening others. This is quite a different process, which will be separately discussed at a later stage.

———

We can now explain more exactly the purport of the definition of the good life with which this chapter began. When I said that the good life consists of love guided by knowledge, the desire which prompted me was the desire to live such a life as far as possible, and to see others living it; and the logical content of the statement is that, in a community where men live in this way, more desires will be satisfied than in one where there is less love or less knowledge. I do not mean that such a life is 'virtuous' or that its opposite is 'sinful', for these are conceptions which seem to me to have no scientific justification.

3

MORAL RULES

The practical need of morals arises from the conflict of desires, whether of different people or of the same person at different times or even at one time. A man desires to drink, and also to be fit for his work next morning. We think him immoral if he adopts the course which gives him the smaller total satisfaction of desire. We think ill of people who are extravagant or reckless, even if they injure no one but themselves. Bentham supposed that the whole of morality could be derived from 'enlightened self-interest', and that a person who always acted with a view to his own maximum satisfaction in the long run would always act rightly. I cannot accept this view. Tyrants have existed who derived exquisite pleasure from watching the infliction of torture; I cannot praise such men when prudence led them to spare their victims' lives with a view to further sufferings another day. Nevertheless, other things being equal, prudence is a part of the good life. Even Robinson Crusoe had occasion to practise industry, self-control and foresight which must be reckoned as moral qualities, since they increased his total satisfaction without counterbalancing injury to others. This part of morals plays a great part in the training of young children, who have little inclination to think of the future. If it were more practised in later life, the world would quickly become a paradise, since it would be quite sufficient to prevent wars, which are acts of passion, not reason. Nevertheless, in spite of the importance of prudence, it is not the most interesting part of morals. Nor is it the part that raises intellectual problems, since it does not require an appeal to anything beyond self-interest.

The part of morality that is not included in prudence, is, in essence, analogous to law, or the rules of a club. It is a method of enabling men to live together in a community in spite of the possibility that their desires may conflict. But here two very different methods are possible. There is the method of criminal law, which aims at a merely external harmony by attaching disagreeable consequences to acts which thwart other men's desires in certain ways. This is also the method of social censure: to be thought ill of by one's own society is a form of punishment, to avoid which most people avoid being known to transgress the code of their set. But there is another method, more fundamental, and far more satisfactory when it succeeds. This is to alter men's characters and desires in such a way as to minimise occasions of conflict by making the success of one man's desires as far as possible consistent with that of another's. That is why love is better than hate, because it brings harmony instead of conflict into the desires of the person concerned. Two people between whom there is love succeed or fail together, but when two people hate each other the success of either is the failure of the other.

If we were right in saying that the good life is inspired by love and guided by knowledge, it is clear that the moral code of any community is not ultimate and self-sufficient, but must be examined with a view to seeing whether it is such as wisdom and benevolence would have decreed. Moral codes have not always been faultless. The Aztecs considered it their painful duty to eat human flesh for fear the light of the sun should grow dim. They erred in their science; and perhaps they would have perceived the scientific error if they had had any love for the sacrificial victims. Some tribes immure girls in the dark from the age of 10 to the age of 17, for fear the sun's rays should render them pregnant. But surely our modern codes of morals contain nothing analogous to these savage practices? Surely we only forbid things which are really harmful, or at any rate so abominable that no decent person could defend them? I am not so sure.

Current morality is a curious blend of utilitarianism and superstition, but the superstitious part has the stronger hold, as is natural, since superstition is the origin of moral rules. Originally, certain acts were thought displeasing to the gods, and were forbidden by law because the divine wrath was apt to descend upon the community, not merely upon the guilty individuals. Hence arose the conception of sin, as that which is displeasing to God. No reason can be assigned as to why certain acts should be thus displeasing; it would be very difficult to say, for instance, why it was displeasing that the kid should be seethed in its mother's milk. But it was known by Revelation that this was the case. Sometimes the Divine commands have been curiously interpreted. For example,

19

we are told not to work on Saturdays, and Protestants take this to mean that we are not to play on Sundays. But the same sublime authority is attributed to the new prohibition as to the old.

It is evident that a man with a scientific outlook on life cannot let himself be intimidated by texts of Scripture or by the teaching of the Church. He will not be content to say 'such-and-such an act is sinful, and that ends the matter'. He will inquire whether it does any harm or whether, on the contrary, the belief that it is sinful does harm. And he will find that, especially in what concerns sex, our current morality contains a very great deal of which the origin is purely superstitious. He will find also that this superstition, like that of the Aztecs, involves needless cruelty, and would be swept away if people were actuated by kindly feelings towards their neighbours. But the defenders of traditional morality are seldom people with warm hearts, as may be seen from the love of militarism displayed by Church dignitaries. One is tempted to think that they value morals as affording a legitimate outlet for their desire to inflict pain; the sinner is fair game, and therefore away with tolerance!

Let us follow an ordinary human life from conception to the grave, and note the points where superstitious morals inflict preventable suffering. I begin with conception, because here the influence of superstition is particularly noteworthy. If the parents are not married, the child has a stigma, as clearly undeserved as anything could be. If either of the parents has venereal disease, the child is likely to inherit it. If they already have too many children for the family income, there will be poverty, underfeeding, overcrowding, very likely incest. Yet the great majority of moralists agree that the parents had better not know how to prevent this misery by preventing conception.[1] To please these moralists, a life of torture is inflicted upon millions of human beings who ought never to have existed, merely because it is supposed that sexual intercourse is wicked unless accompanied by desire for offspring, but not wicked when this desire is present, even though the offspring is humanly certain to be wretched. To be killed suddenly and then eaten, which was the fate of the Aztecs' victims, is a far less degree of suffering than is inflicted upon a child born in miserable surroundings and tainted with venereal disease. Yet it is the greater suffering which is deliberately inflicted by bishops and politicians in the name of morality. If they had even the smallest spark of love or pity for children they could not adhere to a moral code involving this fiendish cruelty.

At birth, and in early infancy, the average child suffers more from economic causes than from superstition. When well-to-do women have children, they have the best doctors, the best nurses, the best diet, the best rest and the best exercise. Working-class women do not enjoy these advantages, and frequently their children die for lack of them. A little is done by the public authorities in the way of care of mothers, but very grudgingly. At a moment when the supply of milk to nursing mothers is being cut down to save expense, public authorities will spend vast sums on paving rich residential districts where there is little traffic. They must know that in taking this decision they are condemning a certain number of

---

[1] This is fortunately no longer true. The vast majority of Protestant and Jewish leaders do not now object to birth control. Russell's statement is a perfectly accurate description of conditions in 1925. It is also significant that, with one or two exceptions, all the great pioneers of contraception – Francis Place, Richard Carlile, Charles Knowlton, Charles Bradlaugh and Margaret Sanger – were prominent Freethinkers. (Editor's note.)

working-class children to death for the crime of poverty. Yet the ruling party are supported by the immense majority of ministers of religion, who, with the Pope at their head, have pledged the vast forces of superstition throughout the world to the support of social injustice.

In all stages of education the influence of superstition is disastrous. A certain percentage of children have the habit of thinking; one of the aims of education is to cure them of this habit. Inconvenient questions are met with 'hush, hush', or with punishment. Collective emotion is used to instil certain kinds of belief, more particularly nationalistic kinds. Capitalists, militarists, and ecclesiastics co-operate in education, because all depend for their power upon the prevalence of emotionalism and the rarity of critical judgement. With the aid of human nature, education succeeds in increasing and intensifying these propensities of the average man.

Another way in which superstition damages education is through its influence on the choice of teachers. For economic reasons, a woman teacher must not be married; for moral reasons, she must not have extra-marital sexual relations. And yet everybody who has taken the trouble to study morbid psychology knows that prolonged virginity is, as a rule, extraordinarily harmful to women, so harmful that, in a sane society, it would be severely discouraged in teachers. The restrictions imposed lead more and more to a refusal, on the part of energetic and enterprising women, to enter the teaching profession. This is all due to the lingering influence of superstitious asceticism.

At middle and upper class schools the matter is even worse. There are chapel services, and the care of morals is in the hands of clergymen. Clergymen, almost necessarily, fail in two ways as teachers of morals. They condemn acts which do not harm and they condone acts which do great harm. They all condemn sexual relations between unmarried people who are fond of each other but not yet sure that they wish to live together all their lives. Most of them condemn birth control. None of them condemns the brutality of a husband who causes his wife to die of too frequent pregnancies. I knew a fashionable clergyman whose wife had nine children in nine years. The doctors told him that if she had another she would die. Next year she had another and died. No one condemned; he retained his benefice and married again. So long as clergymen continue to condone cruelty and condemn innocent pleasure, they can only do harm as guardians of the morals of the young.

Another bad effect of superstition on education is the absence of instruction about the facts of sex. The main physiological facts ought to be taught quite simply and naturally before puberty at a time when they are not exciting. At puberty, the elements of an unsuperstitious sexual morality ought to be taught. Boys and girls should be taught that nothing can justify sexual intercourse unless there is mutual inclination. This is contrary to the teaching of the Church, which holds that, provided the parties are married and the man desires another child, sexual intercourse is justified however great may be the reluctance of the wife. Boys and girls should be taught respect for each other's liberty; they should be made to feel that nothing gives one human being rights over another, and that jealousy and possessiveness kill love. They should be taught that to bring another human being into the world is a very serious matter, only to be undertaken when the child will have a reasonable prospect of health, good surroundings, and parental care. But they should also be taught methods of birth control, so as to insure that children shall only come when they are wanted. Finally, they should be taught the dangers of venereal disease, and the methods of prevention and cure. The increase of human happiness to be expected from sex education on these lines is immeasurable.

It should be recognised that, in the absence of children, sexual relations are a purely private matter, which does not concern either the State or the neighbours. Certain forms of sex which do not lead to children are at present punished by the criminal law: this is purely superstitious, since the matter is one which affects no one except the parties directly concerned. Where there are children, it is a mistake to suppose that it is necessarily to their interest to make divorce very difficult. Habitual drunkenness, cruelty, insanity are grounds upon which divorce is necessary for the children's sake quite as much as for the sake of the wife or husband. The peculiar importance attached, at present, to adultery is quite irrational. It is obvious that many forms of misconduct are more fatal to married happiness than an occasional infidelity. Masculine insistence on a child a year, which is not conventionally misconduct or cruelty, is the most fatal of all.

Moral rules ought not to be such as to make instinctive happiness impossible. Yet that is an effect of strict monogamy in a community where the numbers of the two sexes are very unequal. Of course, under such circumstances, the moral rules are infringed. But when the rules are such that they can only be obeyed by greatly diminishing the happiness of the community, and when it is better they should be infringed than observed, surely it is time that the rules were changed. If this is not done, many people who are acting in a way not contrary to the public interest are faced with the undeserved alternative of hypocrisy or obloquy. The Church does not mind hypocrisy, which is a flattering tribute to its power; but elsewhere it has come to be recognised as an evil which we ought not lightly to inflict.

Even more harmful than theological superstition is the superstition of nationalism, of duty to one's own State and to no other. But I do not propose on this occasion to discuss the matter beyond pointing out that limitation to one's compatriots is contrary to the principle of love which we recognised as constituting the good life. It is also, of course, contrary to enlightened self-interest, since an exclusive nationalism does not pay even the victorious nations.

One other respect in which our society suffers from the theological conception of 'sin' is the treatment of criminals. The view that criminals are 'wicked' and 'deserve' punishment is not one which a rational morality can support. Undoubtedly certain people do things which society wishes to prevent, and does right in preventing as far as possible. We may take murder as the plainest case. Obviously, if a community is to hold together and we are to enjoy its pleasures and advantages, we cannot allow people to kill each other whenever they feel an impulse to do so. But this problem should be treated in a purely scientific spirit. We should ask simply: What is the best method of preventing murder? Of two methods which are equally effective in preventing murder, the one involving least harm to the murderer is to be preferred. The harm to the murderer is wholly regrettable, like the pain of a surgical operation. It may be equally necessary, but it is not a subject for rejoicing. The vindictive feeling called 'moral indignation' is merely a form of cruelty. Suffering to the criminal can never be justified by the notion of vindictive punishment. If education combined with kindness is equally effective, it is to be preferred; still more is it to be preferred if it is more effective. Of course, the prevention of crime and the punishment of crime are two different questions; the object of causing pain to the criminal is presumably deterrent. If prisons were so humanised that a prisoner got a good education for nothing, people might commit crimes in order to qualify for entrance. No doubt prison must be less pleasant than freedom; but the best way to secure this result is to make freedom more pleasant than it sometimes is at present. I do not wish, however, to embark upon the subject of Penal Reform. I merely wish to suggest that we should treat the criminal as we treat a man suffering from plague. Each is a public danger, each must have his liberty curtailed until he has ceased to be a danger. But the man suffering from plague is an object of sympathy and commiseration, whereas the criminal is an object of execration. This is quite irrational. And it is because of this difference of attitude that our prisons are so much less successful in curing criminal tendencies than our hospitals are in curing disease.

4

SALVATION

Individual and social

One of the defects of traditional religion is its individualism, and this defect belongs also to the morality associated with it. Traditionally, the religious life was, as it were, a duologue between the soul and God. To obey the will of God was virtue; and this was possible for the individual quite regardless of the state of the community. Protestant sects developed the idea of 'finding salvation', but it was always present in Christian teaching. This individualism of the separate soul had its value at certain stages of history, but in the modern world we need rather a social than an individual conception of welfare. I want to consider, in this section, how this affects our conception of the good life.

Christianity arose in the Roman Empire among populations, wholly destitute of political power, whose national States had been destroyed and merged in a vast impersonal aggregate. During the first three centuries of the Christian era the individuals who adopted Christianity could not alter the social or political institutions under which they lived, although they were profoundly convinced of their badness. In these circumstances, it was natural that they should adopt the belief that an individual may be perfect in an imperfect world, and that the good life has nothing to do with this world. What I mean may become plain by comparison with Plato's Republic. When Plato wanted to describe the good life, he described a whole community, not an individual; he did so in order to define justice, which is an essentially social conception. He was accustomed to citizenship of a republic, and political responsibility was something which he took for granted. With the loss of Greek freedom comes the rise of Stoicism, which is like Christianity, and unlike Plato, in having an individualistic conception of the good life.

We, who belong to great democracies, should find a more appropriate morality in free Athens than in despotic Imperial Rome. In India, where the political circumstances are very similar to those of Judea in the time of Christ, we find Gandhi preaching a very similar morality to Christ's and being punished for it by the christianised successors of Pontius Pilate. But the more extreme Indian nationalists are not content with individual salvation: they want national salvation. In this they have taken on the outlook of the free democracies of the West. I want to suggest some respects in which this outlook, owing to Christian influences, is not yet sufficiently bold and self-conscious, but is still hampered by the belief in individual salvation.

28

The good life, as we conceive it, demands a multitude of social conditions, and cannot be realised without them. The good life, we said, is a life inspired by love and guided by knowledge. The knowledge required can only exist where governments or millionaires devote themselves to its discovery and diffusion. For example, the spread of cancer is alarming – what are we to do about it? At the moment, no one can answer the question for lack of knowledge; and the knowledge is not likely to emerge except through endowed research. Again, knowledge of science, history, literature and art ought to be attainable by all who desire it; this requires elaborate arrangements on the part of public authorities, and is not to be achieved by means of religious conversion. Then there is foreign trade, without which half the inhabitants of Great Britain would starve; and if we were starving very few of us would live the good life. It is needless to multiply examples. The important point is that, in all that differentiates between a good life and a bad one, the world is a unity, and the man who pretends to live independently is a conscious or unconscious parasite.

The idea of individual salvation, with which the early Christians consoled themselves for their political subjection, becomes impossible as soon as we escape from a very narrow conception of the good life. In the orthodox Christian conception, the good life is the virtuous life, and virtue consists in obedience to the will of God, and the will of God is revealed to each individual through the voice of conscience. This whole conception is that of men subject to an alien despotism. The good life involves much beside virtue – intelligence, for instance. And conscience is a most fallacious guide, since it consists of vague reminiscences of precepts heard in early youth, so that it is never wiser than its possessor's nurse or mother. To live a good life in the fullest sense a man must have a good education, friends, love, children (if he desires them), a sufficient income to keep him from want and grave anxiety, good health, and work which is not uninteresting. All these things, in varying degrees, depend upon the community, and are helped or hindered by political events. The good life must be lived in a good society, and is not fully possible otherwise.

This is the fundamental defect of the aristocratic ideal. Certain good things, such as art and science and friendship, can flourish very well in an aristocratic society. They existed in Greece on a basis of slavery; they exist among ourselves on a basis of exploitation. But love, in the form of sympathy, or benevolence, cannot exist freely in an aristocratic society. The aristocrat has to persuade himself that the slave or proletarian or coloured man is of inferior clay, and that his sufferings do not matter. At the present moment, polished English gentlemen flog Africans so severely that they die after hours of unspeakable anguish. Even if these gentlemen are well-educated, artistic, and admirable conversationalists, I cannot admit that they are living the good life. Human nature imposes some limitation of sympathy, but not such a degree as that. In a democratically-minded society, only a maniac would behave in this way. The limitation of sympathy involved in the aristocratic ideal is its condemnation. Salvation is an aristocratic ideal, because it is individualistic. For this reason, also, the idea of personal salvation, however interpreted and expanded, cannot serve for the definition of the good life.

Another characteristic of salvation is that it results from a catastrophic change, like the conversion of St Paul. Shelley's poems afford an illustration of this conception applied to societies; the moment comes when everybody is converted, the 'anarchs' fly, and 'the world's great age begins anew'. It may be said that a poet is an unimportant person, whose ideas are of no consequence. But I am persuaded that a large proportion of revolutionary leaders have had ideas extremely like Shelley's. They have thought that misery and cruelty and degradation were due to tyrants or priests or capitalists or Germans, and that if these sources of evil were overthrown there would be a general change of heart and we should all live happy ever after. Holding these beliefs, they have been willing to wage a 'war to end war'. Comparatively fortunate were those who had suffered defeat or death; those who had the misfortune to emerge victorious were reduced to cynicism and despair by the failure of all their glowing hopes. The ultimate source of these hopes was the Christian doctrine of catastrophic conversion as the road to salvation.

I do not wish to suggest that revolutions are never necessary, but I do wish to suggest that they are not short cuts to the millennium. There is no short cut to the good life, whether individual or social. To build up the good life, we must build up intelligence, self-control and sympathy. This is a quantitative matter, a matter of gradual improvement, of early training, of educational experiment. Only impatience prompts the belief in the possibility of sudden improvement. The gradual improvement that is possible, and the methods by which it may be achieved, are a matter for future science. But something can be said now. Some part of what can be said I shall try to indicate in a final section.

5

SCIENCE AND HAPPINESS

The purpose of the moralist is to improve men's behaviour. This is a laudable ambition, since their behaviour is for the most part deplorable. But I cannot praise the moralist either for the particular improvements he desires or for the methods he adopts for achieving them. His ostensible method is moral exhortation; his real method (if he is orthodox) is a system of economic rewards and punishments. The former effects nothing permanent or important; the influence of revivalists, from Savonarola downwards, has always been very transitory. The latter – the rewards and punishments – have a very considerable effect. They cause a man, for example, to prefer casual prostitutes to a quasi-permanent mistress, because it is necessary to adopt the method which is most easily concealed. They thus keep up the numbers of a very dangerous profession, and secure the prevalence of venereal disease. These are not the objects desired by the moralist, and he is too unscientific to notice that they are the objects which he actually achieves.

Is there anything better to be substituted for this unscientific mixture of preaching and bribery? I think there is.

Men's actions are harmful either from ignorance or from bad desires. 'Bad' desires, when we are speaking from a social point of view, may be defined as those which tend to thwart the desires of others, or more exactly, those which thwart more desires than they assist. It is not necessary to dwell upon the harmfulness that springs from ignorance; here, more knowledge is all that is wanted, so that the road to improvement lies in more research and more education. But the harmfulness that springs from bad desires is a more difficult matter.

In the ordinary man and woman there is a certain amount of active malevolence, both special ill-will directed to particular enemies and general impersonal pleasure in the misfortunes of others. It is customary to cover this over with fine phrases; about half of conventional morality is a cloak for it. But it must be faced if the moralists' aim of improving our actions is to be achieved. It is shown in a thousand ways, great and small: in the glee with which people repeat and believe scandal, in the unkind treatment of criminals in spite of clear proof that better treatment would have more effect in reforming them, in the unbelievable barbarity with which all white races treat Negroes, and in the gusto with which old ladies and clergymen pointed out the duty of military service to young men during the War. Even children may be the objects of wanton cruelty: David Copperfield and Oliver Twist are by no means imaginary. This active malevolence is the worst feature of human nature and the one which it is most necessary to change if the world is to grow happier. Probably this one cause has more to do with war than all the economic and political causes put together.

Given this problem of preventing malevolence, how shall we deal with it? First let us try to understand its causes. These are, I think, partly social, partly physiological. The world, now as much as at any former time, is based upon life-and-death competition; the question at issue in the War was whether German or Allied children should die of want and starvation. (Apart from malevolence on both sides there was not the slightest reason why both should not survive.) Most people have in the background of their minds a haunting fear of ruin; this is especially true of people who have children. The rich fear that Bolsheviks will confiscate their investments; the poor fear that they will lose their job or their health. Everyone is engaged in the frantic pursuit of 'security' and imagines that this is to be achieved by keeping potential enemies in subjection. It is in moments of panic that cruelty becomes most widespread and most atrocious. Reactionaries everywhere appeal to fear: in England, to fear of Bolshevism; in France, to fear of Germany; in Germany, to fear of France. And the sole effect of their appeals is to increase the danger against which they wish to be protected.

It must, therefore, be one of the chief concerns of the scientific moralist to combat fear. This can be done in two ways: by increasing security, and by cultivating courage. I am speaking of fear as an irrational passion, not of the rational prevision of possible misfortune. When a theatre catches fire, the rational man foresees disaster just as clearly as the man stricken with panic, but he adopts methods likely to diminish the disaster, whereas the man stricken with panic increases it. Europe since 1914 has been like a panic-stricken audience in a theatre on fire; what is needed is calm, authoritative

34

directions as to how to escape without trampling each other to pieces in the process. The Victorian Age, for all its humbug, was a period of rapid progress, because men were dominated by hope rather than fear. If we are again to have progress, we must again be dominated by hope.

Everything that increases the general security is likely to diminish cruelty. This applies to prevention of war, whether through the instrumentality of the League of Nations or otherwise; to prevention of destitution; to better health by improvement in medicine, hygiene, and sanitation; and to all other methods of lessening the terrors that lurk in the abysses of men's minds and emerge as nightmares when they sleep. But nothing is accomplished by an attempt to make a portion of mankind secure at the expense of another portion – Frenchmen at the expense of Germans, capitalists at the expense of wage-earners, white men at the expense of yellow men, and so on. Such methods only increase terror in the dominant group, lest just resentment should lead the oppressed to rebel. Only justice can give security; and by 'justice' I mean the recognition of the equal claims of all human beings.

In addition to social changes designed to bring security there is, however, another and more direct means of diminishing fear, namely by a regimen designed to increase courage. Owing to the importance of courage in battle, men early discovered means of increasing it by education and diet – eating human flesh, for example, was supposed to be useful. But military courage was to be the prerogative of the ruling caste: Spartans were to have more than helots, British officers than Indian privates, men than women, and so on. For centuries it was supposed to be the privilege of the aristocracy. Every increase of courage in the ruling caste was used to increase the burdens on the oppressed, and therefore to increase the grounds for fear in the oppressors, and therefore to leave the causes of cruelty undiminished. Courage must be democratised before it can make men humane.

To a great extent, courage has already been democratised by recent events. The suffragettes showed that they possessed as much courage as the bravest men; this demonstration was essential in winning them the vote. The common soldier in the War needed as much courage as a captain or lieutenant, and much more than a general; this had much to do with his lack of servility after demobilisation. The Bolsheviks, who proclaim themselves the champions of the proletariat, are not lacking in courage, whatever else may be said of them; this is proved by their pre-revolutionary record. In Japan, where formerly the Samurai had a monopoly of martial ardour, conscription brought the need of courage throughout the male population. Thus among all the Great Powers much has been done during the past half-century to make courage no longer an aristocratic monopoly: if this were not the case, the danger to democracy would be far greater than it is.

But courage in fighting is by no means the only form, nor perhaps even the most important. There is courage in facing poverty, courage in facing derision, courage in facing the hostility of one's own herd. In these, the bravest soldiers are often lamentably deficient. And above all there is the courage to think calmly and rationally in the face of danger, and to control the impulse of panic fear or panic rage. These are certainly things which education can help to give. And the teaching of every form of courage is rendered easier by good health, good physique, adequate nourishment, and free play for fundamental vital impulses. Perhaps the physiological sources of courage could be discovered by comparing the blood of a cat with that of a rabbit. In all likelihood there is no limit to what science could do in the way of increasing courage, by example, experience of danger, an athletic life, and a suitable diet. All these things our upper class boys to a great extent enjoy, but as yet they are in the main the prerogative of wealth. The courage so far encouraged in the poorer sections of the community is courage under orders, not the kind that involves initiative and leadership. When the qualities that now confer leadership have become universal, there will no longer be leaders and followers, and democracy will have been realised at last.

But fear is not the only source of malevolence; envy and disappointment also have their share. The envy of cripples and hunchbacks is proverbial as a source of malignity, but other misfortunes than theirs produce similar results. A man or woman who has been thwarted sexually is apt to be full of envy; this generally takes the form of moral condemnation of the more fortunate. Much of the driving force of revolutionary movements is due to envy of the rich. Jealousy is, of course, a special form of envy – envy of love. The old often envy the young; when they do, they are apt to treat them cruelly.

There is, so far as I know, no way of dealing with envy except to make the lives of the envious happier and fuller, and to encourage in youth the idea of collective enterprises rather than competition. The worst forms of envy are in those who have not had a full life in the way of marriage, or children, or career. Such misfortunes could in most cases be avoided by better social institutions. Still, it must be admitted that a residuum of envy is likely to remain. There are many instances in history of generals so jealous of each other that they preferred defeat to enhancement of the other's reputation. Two politicians of the same party, or two artists of the same school, are almost sure to be jealous of one another. In such cases, there seems nothing to be done except to arrange, as far as possible, that each competitor shall be unable to injure the other, and shall only be able to win by superior merit. An artist's jealousy of a rival does little harm usually, because the only effective way of indulging it is to paint better pictures than his rival's, since it is not open to him to destroy his rival's pictures. Where envy is unavoidable it must be used as a stimulus to one's own efforts, not to the thwarting of the efforts of rivals.

The possibilities of science in the way of increasing human happiness are not confined to diminishing those aspects of human nature which make for mutual defeat, and which we therefore call 'bad'. There is probably no limit to what science can do in the way of increasing positive excellence. Health has already been greatly improved; in spite of the lamentations of those who idealise the past, we live longer and have fewer illnesses than any class or nation in the eighteenth century. With a little more application of the knowledge we already possess, we might be much healthier than we are. And future discoveries are likely to accelerate this process enormously.

So far, it has been physical science that has had most effect upon our lives, but in the future physiology and psychology are likely to be far more potent. When we have discovered how character depends upon physiological conditions, we shall be able, if we choose, to produce far more of the type of human being that we admire. Intelligence, artistic capacity, benevolence – all these things no doubt could be increased by science. There seems scarcely any limit to what *could* be done in the way of producing a good world, if only men would use science wisely. I have expressed elsewhere my fears that men may not make a wise use of the power they derive from science.[1] At present I am concerned with the good that men could do if they chose, not with the question whether they will choose rather to do harm.

There is a certain attitude about the application of science to human life with which I have some sympathy, though I do not, in the last analysis, agree with it. It is the attitude of those who dread what is 'unnatural'. Rousseau is, of course, the great protagonist of this view in Europe. In Asia, Lao-Tze has set it forth even more persuasively, and 2400 years sooner. I think there is a mixture of truth and falsehood in the admiration of 'nature', which it is important to disentangle. To begin with, what is 'natural'? Roughly speaking, anything to which the speaker was accustomed in childhood. Lao-Tze objects to roads and carriages and boats, all of which were probably unknown in the village where he was born. Rousseau has got used to these things, and does not regard them as against nature. But he would no doubt have thundered against railways if he had lived to see them. Clothes and cooking are too ancient to be denounced by most of the apostles of nature, though they all object to new fashions in either. Birth control is thought wicked by people who tolerate celibacy, because the former is a new violation of nature and the latter an ancient one. In all these ways those who preach 'nature' are inconsistent, and one is tempted to regard them as mere conservatives.

Nevertheless, there is something to be said in their favour. Take for instance vitamins, the discovery of which has produced a revulsion in favour of 'natural' foods. It seems,

[1] See *Icarus*.

39

however, that vitamins can be supplied by cod liver oil and electric light, which are certainly not part of the 'natural' diet of a human being. This case illustrates that, in the absence of knowledge, unexpected harm may be done by a new departure from nature; but when the harm has come to be understood it can usually be remedied by some new artificiality. As regards our physical environment and our physical means of gratifying our desires, I do not think the doctrine of 'nature' justifies anything beyond a certain experimental caution in the adoption of new expedients. Clothes, for instance, are contrary to nature, and need to be supplemented by another unnatural practice, namely washing, if they are not to bring disease. But the two practices together make a man healthier than the savage who eschews both.

There is more to be said for 'nature' in the realm of human desires. To force upon man, woman or child a life which thwarts their strongest impulses is both cruel and dangerous; in this sense, a life according to 'nature' is to be commended with certain provisos. Nothing could be more artificial than an underground electric railway, but no violence is done to a child's nature when it is taken to travel in one; on the contrary, almost all children find the experience delightful. Artificialities which gratify the desires of ordinary human beings are good, other things being equal. But there is nothing to be said for ways of life which are artificial in the sense of being imposed by authority or economic necessity. Such ways of life are, no doubt, to some extent necessary at present; ocean travel would become very difficult if there were no stokers on steamers. But necessities of this kind are regrettable, and we ought to look for ways of avoiding them. A certain amount of work is not a thing to complain of; indeed, in nine cases out of ten, it makes a man happier than complete idleness. But the amount and kind of work that most people have to do at present is a grave evil: especially bad is the life-long bondage to routine. Life should not be too closely regulated or too methodical; our impulses, when not positively destructive or injurious to others, ought if possible to have free play; there should be room for adventure. Human nature we should respect, because our impulses and desires are the stuff out of which our happiness is to be made. It is no use to give men something abstractedly considered 'good'; we must give them something desired or needed if we are to add to their happiness. Science may learn in time to mould our desires so that they shall not conflict with those of other people to the same extent as they do now; then we shall be able to satisfy a larger proportion of our desires than at present. In that sense, but in that sense only, our desires will then have become 'better'. A single desire is no better and no worse, considered in isolation, than any other; but a group of desires is better than another group if all of the first group can be satisfied simultaneously, while in the second group some are inconsistent with others. That is why love is better than hatred.

To respect physical nature is foolish; physical nature should be studied with a view to making it serve human ends as far as possible, but it remains ethically neither good nor bad. And where physical nature and human nature interact, as in the population question, there is no need to fold our hands in passive adoration and accept war, pestilence and famine as the only possible means of dealing with excessive fertility. The divines say: it is wicked, in this matter, to apply science to the physical side of the problem; we must (they say) apply morals to the human side and practise abstinence. Apart from the fact that everyone, including the divines, knows that their advice will not be taken, why should it be wicked to solve the population question by adopting physical means for preventing conception? No answer is forthcoming except one based upon antiquated dogmas. And clearly the violence to nature advocated by the divines is at least as great as that involved in birth control. The divines prefer a violence to human nature, which, when successfully practised, involves unhappiness, envy, a tendency to persecution, often madness. I prefer a 'violence' to physical nature which is of the same sort as that involved in the steam engine or even in the use of an umbrella. This instance shows how ambiguous and uncertain is the application of the principle that we should follow 'nature'.

Nature, even human nature, will cease more and more to be an absolute datum; more and more it will become what scientific manipulation has made it. Science can, if it chooses, enable our grandchildren to live the good life, by giving them knowledge, self-control, and characters productive of harmony rather than strife. At present it is teaching our children to kill each other, because many men of science are willing to sacrifice the future of mankind to their own momentary prosperity. But this phase will pass when men have acquired the same domination over their own passions that they already have over the physical forces of the external world. Then at last we shall have won our freedom.

HOW I WRITE

I cannot pretend to know how writing ought to be done, or what a wise critic would advise me to do with a view to improving my own writing. The most that I can do is to relate some things about my own attempts.

Until I was twenty-one, I wished to write more or less in the style of John Stuart Mill. I liked the structure of his sentences and his manner of developing a subject. I had, however, already a different ideal, derived, I suppose, from mathematics. I wished to say everything in the smallest number of words in which it could be said clearly. Perhaps, I thought, one should imitate Baedeker rather than any more literary model. I would spend hours trying to find the shortest way of saying something without ambiguity, and to this aim I was willing to sacrifice all attempts at aesthetic excellence.

At the age of twenty-one, however, I came under a new influence, that of my future brother-in-law, Logan Pearsall

Smith. He was at that time exclusively interested in style as opposed to matter. His gods were Flaubert and Walter Pater, and I was quite ready to believe that the way to learn how to write was to copy their technique. He gave me various simple rules, of which I remember only two: 'Put a comma every four words', and 'never use "and" except at the beginning of a sentence.' His most emphatic advice was that one must always re-write. I conscientiously tried this, but found that my first draft was almost always better than my second. This discovery has saved me an immense amount of time. I do not, of course, apply it to the substance, but only to the form. When I discover an error of an important kind, I re-write the whole. What I do not find is that I can improve a sentence when I am satisfied with what it means.

Very gradually I have discovered ways of writing with a minimum of worry and anxiety. When I was young each fresh piece of serious work used to seem to me for a time—perhaps a long time—to be beyond my powers. I would fret myself into a nervous state from fear that it was never going to come right. I would make one unsatisfying attempt after another, and in the end have to discard them all. At last I found that such fumbling attempts were a waste of time. It appeared that after first contemplating a book on some subject, and after giving serious preliminary attention to it, I needed a period of subconscious incubation which could not be hurried and was, if anything, impeded by deliberate thinking. Sometimes I would find, after a time, that I had made a mistake, and that I could not write the book I had had in mind. But often I was more fortunate. Having, by a time of very intense concentration, planted the problem in my subconsciousness, it would germinate underground until, suddenly, the solution emerged with blinding clarity, so that it only remained to write down what had appeared as if in a revelation.

The most curious example of this process, and the one which led me subsequently to rely upon it, occurred at the beginning of 1914. I had undertaken to give the Lowell Lectures at Boston, and had chosen as my subject 'Our Knowledge of the External World'. Throughout 1913 I thought about this topic. In term time in my rooms at Cambridge, in vacations in a quiet inn on the upper reaches of the Thames, I concentrated with such intensity that I sometimes forgot to breathe and emerged panting as from a trance. But all to no avail. To every theory that I could think of I could perceive fatal objections. At last, in despair, I went off to Rome for Christmas, hoping that a holiday would revive my flagging energy. I got back to Cambridge on the last day of 1913, and although my difficulties were still completely unresolved I arranged, because the remaining time was short, to dictate as best as I could to a stenographer. Next morning, as she came in at the door, I suddenly saw exactly what I had to say, and proceeded to dictate the whole book without a moment's hesitation.

I do not want to convey an exaggerated impression. The book was very imperfect, and I now think that it contains serious errors. But it was the best that I could have done at that time, and a more leisurely method (within the time at my disposal) would almost certainly have produced something worse. Whatever may be true of other people, this is the right method for me. Flaubert and Pater, I have found, are best forgotten so far as I am concerned.

Although what I now think about how to write is not so very different from what I thought at the age of eighteen, my development has not been by any means rectilinear. There was a time, in the first years of this century, when I had more florid and rhetorical ambitions. This was the time when I wrote *A Free Man's Worship*, a work of which I do not now think well. At that time I was steeped in Milton's prose, and his rolling periods reverberated through the caverns of my mind. I cannot say that I no longer admire them, but for me to imitate them involves a certain insincerity. In fact, all imitation is dangerous. Nothing could be better in style than the Prayer Book and the Authorized Version of the Bible, but they express a way of thinking and feeling which is different from that of our time. A style is not good unless it is an intimate and almost involuntary expression of the personality of the writer, and then only if the writer's personality is worth expressing. But although direct imitation is always to be deprecated, there is much to be gained by familiarity with good prose, especially in cultivating a sense for prose rhythm.

There are some simple maxims—not perhaps quite so simple as those which my brother-in-law Logan Pearsall Smith offered me—which I think might be commended to writers of expository prose. First: never use a long word if a short word will do. Second: if you want to make a statement with a great many qualifications, put some of the qualifications in separate sentences. Third: do not let the beginning of your sentence lead the reader to an expectation which is contradicted by the end. Take, say, such a sentence as the following, which might occur in a work on sociology: 'Human beings are completely exempt from undesirable behaviour-patterns only when certain prerequisites, not satisfied except in a small percentage of actual cases, have, through some fortuitous concourse of favourable circumstances, whether congenital or environmental, chanced to combine in producing an individual in whom many factors deviate from the norm in a socially advantageous manner.' Let us see if we can translate this sentence into English. I suggest the following: 'All men are scoundrels, or at any rate almost all. The men who are not must have had unusual luck, both in their birth and in their upbringing.' This is shorter and more intelligible, and says just the same thing. But I am afraid any professor who used the second sentence instead of the first would get the sack.

This suggests a word of advice to such of my hearers as may happen to be professors. I am allowed to use plain English because everybody knows that I could use mathematical logic if I chose. Take the statement: 'Some people marry their deceased wives' sisters.' I can express this in language which only becomes intelligible after years of study, and this gives me freedom. I suggest to young professors that their first work should be written in a jargon only to be understood by the erudite few. With that behind them, they can ever after say what they have to say in a language 'understanded of the people'. In these days, when our very lives are at the mercy of the professors, I cannot but think that they would deserve our gratitude if they adopted my advice.

(*Portraits from Memory*, London: Allen & Unwin; New York: Simon & Schuster, 1956.)

WHY I TOOK TO PHILOSOPHY

The motives which have led men to become philosophers have been of various kinds. The most respectable motive was the desire to understand the world. In early days, while philosophy and science were indistinguishable, this motive predominated. Another motive which was a potent incentive in early times was the illusoriness of the senses. Such questions as: where is the rainbow? Are things really what they seem to be in sunshine or in moonlight? In more modern forms of the same problem—are things really what they look like to the naked eye or what they look like through a microscope? Such puzzles, however, very soon came to be supplemented by a larger problem. When the Greeks began to be doubtful about the Gods of Olympus, some of them sought in philosophy a substitute for traditional beliefs. Through the combination of these two motives there arose a twofold movement in philosophy: on the one hand, it was thought to show that much which passes for knowledge in everyday life is not real knowledge; and on the other hand, that there is a deeper philosophical truth which, according to most philosophers, is more consonant than our everyday beliefs with what we should wish the universe to be. In almost all philosophy doubt has been the goad and certainty has been the goal. There has been doubt about the senses, doubt about science, and doubt about theology. In some philosophers one of these has been more prominent, in others another. Philosophers have also differed widely as to the answers they have suggested to these doubts and even as to whether any answers are possible.

All the traditional motives combined to lead me to philosophy, but there were two that specially influenced me. The one which operated first and continued longest was the desire to find some knowledge that could be accepted as certainly true. The other motive was the desire to find some satisfaction for religious impulses.

I think the first thing that led me towards philosophy (though at that time the word 'philosophy' was still unknown to me) occurred at the age of eleven. My childhood was mainly solitary as my only brother was seven years older than I was. No doubt as a result of much solitude I became rather solemn, with a great deal of time for thinking but not much knowledge for my thoughtfulness to exercise itself upon. I had, though I was not yet aware of it, the pleasure in demonstrations which is typical of the mathematical mind. After I grew up I found others who felt as I did on this matter. My friend G. H. Hardy, who was professor of pure mathematics, enjoyed this pleasure in a very high degree. He told me once that if he could find a proof that I was going to die in five minutes he would of course be sorry to lose me, but this sorrow would be quite out-weighed by pleasure in the proof. I entirely sympathized with him and was not at all offended. Before I began the study of geometry somebody had told me that it proved things and this caused me to feel delight when my brother said he would teach it to me. Geometry in those days was still 'Euclid'. My brother began at the beginning with the definitions. These I accepted readily enough. But he came next to the axioms. 'These', he said, 'can't be proved, but they have to be assumed before the rest can be proved.' At these words my hopes crumbled. I had thought it would be wonderful to find something that one could PROVE, and then it turned out that this could only be done by means of assumptions of which there was no proof. I looked at my brother with a sort of indignation and said: 'But why should I admit these things if they can't be proved?' He replied: 'Well, if you won't, we can't go on.' I thought it might be worth-while to learn the rest of the story, so I agreed to admit the axioms for the time being. But I remained full of doubt and perplexity as regards a region in which I had hoped to find indisputable clarity. In spite of these doubts, which at most times I forgot, and which I usually supposed capable of some answer not yet known to me, I found great delight in mathematics—much more delight, in fact, than in any other study. I liked to think of the applications of mathematics to the physical world, and I hoped that in time there would be a mathematics of human behaviour as precise as the mathematics of machines. I hoped this because I liked demonstrations, and at most times this motive outweighed the desire, which I also felt, to believe in free will. Neverthe-less I never quite overcame my fundamental doubts as to the validity of mathematics.

When I began to learn higher mathematics, fresh difficulties assailed me. My teachers offered me proofs which I felt to be fallacious and which, as I learnt later, had been recognized as fallacious. I did not know then, or for some time after I had left Cambridge, that better proofs had been found by German mathematicians. I therefore remained in a receptive mood for the heroic measures of Kant's philosophy. This suggested a large new survey from which such difficulties as had troubled me looked niggling and unimportant. All this I came later on to think wholly fallacious, but that was only after I had allowed myself to sink deep in the mire of metaphysical muddles. I was encouraged in my transition to philosophy by a certain disgust with mathematics, resulting from too much concentration and too much absorption in the sort of skill that is needed in examinations. The attempt to acquire examination technique had led me to think of mathematics as consisting of artful dodges and ingenious devices and as altogether too much like a cross-word puzzle. When, at the end of my first three years at Cambridge, I emerged from my last mathematical examination I swore that I would never look at mathematics again and sold all my mathematical books. In this mood the survey of philosophy gave me all the delight of a new landscape on emerging from a valley.

It had not been only in mathematics that I sought certainty. Like Descartes (whose work was still unknown to me) I thought that my own existence was, to me, indubitable. Like him, I felt it possible to suppose that the outer world is nothing but a dream. But even if it be, it is a dream that is really dreamt, and the fact that I experience it remains unshakably certain. This line of thought occurred to me first when I was sixteen, and I was glad when I learnt later that Descartes had made it the basis of his philosophy.

At Cambridge my interest in philosophy received a stimulus from another motive. The scepticism which had led me to doubt even mathematics had also led me to question the fundamental dogmas of religion, but I ardently desired to find a way of preserving at least something that could be called religious belief. From the age of fifteen to the age of eighteen I spent a great deal of time and thought on religious belief. I examined fundamental dogmas one by one, hoping with all my heart to find some reason for accepting them. I wrote my thoughts in a notebook which I still possess. They were, of course, crude and youthful, but for the moment I saw no answer to the Agnosticism which they suggested. At Cambridge I was made aware of whole systems of thought of which I had previously been ignorant and I abandoned for a time the ideas which I had worked out in solitude. At Cambridge I was introduced to the philosophy of Hegel who, in the course of nineteen abstruse volumes, professed to have proved something which would do quite well as an emended and sophisticated version of traditional beliefs. Hegel thought of the universe as a closely knit unity. His universe was like a jelly in the fact that, if you touched any one part of it, the whole quivered; but it was unlike a jelly in the fact that it could not really be cut up into parts. The appearance of consisting of parts, according to him, was a delusion. The only reality was the Absolute, which was his name for God. In this philosophy I found comfort for a time. As presented to me by its adherents, especially McTaggart, who was then an intimate friend of mine, Hegel's philosophy had seemed both charming and demonstrable. McTaggart was a philosopher some six years senior to me and throughout his life an ardent disciple of Hegel. He influenced his contemporaries very considerably, and I for a time fell under his sway. There was a curious pleasure in making oneself believe that time and space are unreal, that matter is an illusion, and that the world really consists of nothing but mind. In a rash moment, however, I turned from the disciples to the Master and found in Hegel himself a farrago of confusions and what seemed to me little better than puns. I therefore abandoned his philosophy.

For a time I found satisfaction in a doctrine derived, with modification, from Plato. According to Plato's doctrine, which I accepted only in a watered-down form, there is an unchanging timeless world of ideas of which the world presented to our senses is an imperfect copy. Mathematics, according to this doctrine, deals with the world of ideas and has in consequence an exactness and perfection which is absent from the everyday world. This kind of mathematical mysticism, which Plato derived from Pythagoras, appealed to me. But in the end I found myself obliged to abandon this doctrine also, and I have never since found religious satisfaction in any philosophical doctrine that I could accept.

(*Portraits from Memory*, London: Allen & Unwin; New York: Simon & Schuster, 1956.)

INDEX